CHIEF GATI
and the
TALKING WIND
and Other
SHORT STORIES

MARTIN MUGANGA

PAGE PUBLISHING
Conneaut Lake, PA

First originally published by Page Publishing 2024

ISBN 979-8-89315-525-9 (pbk)
ISBN 979-8-89315-539-6 (digital)

Printed in the United States of America

CONTENTS

CHIEF GATI AND THE TALKING WIND

(Part 1)

Once upon a time, in the magnificent Kingdom of Fahi, the youngest son of Chief Tiga was born! It was a day of pure magic and wonder as the entire kingdom rejoiced in the arrival of their new prince. Chief Tiga's precious last born was named Gati, also known as the Son of the Wind, for he came into this world amid a mighty windstorm of epic proportions! The skies opened up with the heaviest rainfall and the strongest winds the kingdom had ever witnessed in nearly a century. Before this incredible storm, there had been a long dry spell, with no rain for months and no great storm for years. As soon as Gati let out his first cry, the fierce storm that had been wreaking havoc on the kingdom suddenly ceased. It was nothing short of a miracle, a divine sign that only a true prince chosen by the gods could bring about. The elders marveled at this extraordinary event and bestowed upon Gati the revered title of the Son of the Wind. They believed that he possessed a unique power to command the very elements themselves. And so with the birth of Gati, a new era of hope and promise dawned upon the Kingdom of Fahi. The people of Fahi celebrated the arrival of Gati with grand festivities that lasted for days on end.

The streets were filled with music, dancing, and feasting as the kingdom basked in the glow of their new prince. Gati grew up to be a wise and compassionate teenager, beloved by all who knew him. His presence brought prosperity and peace to the land, as he used his gift of the wind to protect the kingdom from any harm that threatened its people. The legend of the Son of the Wind spread far and wide, and travelers from distant lands came to witness his power firsthand. Gati's legacy endured for generations, as the Kingdom of Fahi flourished under his benevolent rule, forever grateful for the divine blessing that had been bestowed upon them. Chief Tiga was the seventh king of Fahi, and Gati was the last born among his four children. Gati was a stubborn boy but also very brave in the face of all danger, even from an early age. At sixteen, the Son of the Wind could wrestle with the champion bull in the kingdom known as Libu, whom the villagers believed to be the fiercest bull they had ever seen. Libu was a champion bull that fought and defeated all the bulls in the Fahi Kingdom and all neighboring kingdoms. It was said that Gati would wrestle Libu as if he was eating matooke. What an incredible feat for such a young boy!

Fahi Kingdom was located to the west of Giha Kingdom, and to the far east was a large prison jungle that held prisoners from all neighboring kingdoms. But in the midst of this harsh environment, there was a legend—Dati, the warrior of the jungle! His bravery and strength were unmatched, making him a force to be reckoned with. His martial arts and wrestling skills were so exceptional that even the other prisoners feared and respected him. Dati's reputation spread like wildfire, earning him a legendary status among both inmates and guards. His unwavering courage and determination inspired others to rise up against injustice in the unforgiving jungle prison. Despite facing countless challenges, Dati remained steadfast in his mission to protect and defend his fellow prisoners, becoming a beacon of hope and resilience in the darkest corners of the prison. Dati's story is one of triumph against all odds—a true hero in the most unlikely of places!

When Gati was turning twenty years old, the Fahi Kingdom, still under the chiefdom of Tiga, faced a grave threat as it was occupied by the ruthless Hagi warriors! The Hagi tribe, infamous for their barbaric acts of cannibalism, instilled fear in every kingdom they encountered. In a swift and brutal invasion, the Hagi warriors conquered Fahi, forcing Chief Tiga, his family, the Fahi elders, and the majority of the village's inhabitants to flee in a desperate attempt to escape the clutches of their merciless oppressors. As they embarked on a treacherous journey northward, Chief Tiga's health deteriorated rapidly due to the injuries sustained during the harrowing escape from the Hagi warriors. Tragically, on the fourth night of their journey, as the sun dipped below the horizon, Chief Tiga succumbed to his wounds, leaving his people devastated and grief-stricken by the loss of their beloved leader.

Among those caught by the Hagi warriors was Gati! He found himself a prisoner of war in the famous jungle prison. Fear of death crept into his mind for the first time as he faced the terrifying monsters lurking within the prison, creatures of mysterious origin causing chaos wherever they roamed. But then, a ray of hope appeared in the form of Dati, a kind and compassionate fellow prisoner. Despite his own hardships, Dati showed Gati empathy and understanding. As they bonded, Gati opened up about his harrowing experience of the Hagi's brutal attack on the Fahi Kingdom. At that moment, Dati knew he had to protect Gati from the other menacing prisoners. With a firm handshake and words of encouragement, Dati lifted Gati up, instilling in him a newfound sense of courage and strength. Together, they stood tall, ready to face whatever challenges came their way!

Dati had been in the jungle prison for five years, and he explained to Gati the secret of staying in the jungle prison without being hurt. It was martial arts and wrestling; Dati had survived because of being a master in martial arts. No one in the jungle prison could put him down when it came to fighting. Convinced that Gati could be a strong mentee, Dati asked if he could begin training him in martial arts at sunbreak. Without hesitation, Gati accepted. What remained untold among the two men was that Dati had seen Gati's future in a dream he had the first day Gati was brought into the jungle prison. This dream would forever remain their unspoken bond of brotherhood and hope for the future of the Fahi Kingdom. Little did they know that their shared journey of mastering martial arts would lead them to uncover hidden truths about themselves and their destinies. As the days passed and their training intensified, Gati began to realize the depth of Dati's wisdom and the profound connection they shared. Together, they would not only become skilled fighters but also loyal allies in the battle for the future of their kingdom.

As promised, the very next day, Dati started training Gati at every opportunity. And with each passing day, Gati's skills and abilities continued to improve, making him a formidable student under Dati's guidance. Gati quickly rose to become Dati's most talented pupil, showcasing his prowess by triumphing over various challengers within the prison walls. As Gati honed his focus and sharpened his senses with each fight and lesson, he began to tap into a hidden power—the ability to communicate with the wind that whispered through the jungle prison. With each passing year, Gati's connection to this elemental force grew stronger, allowing him to harness its energy in ways he never thought possible. As the wind whispered the secrets of the jungle to Gati, he learned to control its power and use it to his advantage in battles, becoming a force to be reckoned with among his peers. His mastery over the wind brought him respect and admiration from all who witnessed his extraordinary abilities, solidifying his reputation as a skilled warrior with a unique gift.

Gati and Dati, after spending four long years in jail, finally hatched a daring plan for the perfect escape! With Gati's incredible ability to communicate with the wind, they devised a three-part strategy that relied on the wind's guidance. First, they bravely journeyed to the far east side of the jungle prison, with the wind leading them through treacherous terrain that no one else could navigate. The dense foliage and treacherous paths seemed endless, but Gati's connection with the wind kept them on course, guiding them through the tangled undergrowth and past lurking dangers. Gati fearlessly led the way through the dense jungle, their hearts pounding with anticipation until they finally reached the legendary miracle tree. The mystical Talking Wind instructed them to extract the leaves, squeeze them, and apply the magical substance to their bodies, rendering them invisible to the fearsome Hagi warriors. The liquid, a shimmering substance that seemed to bend and twist light around them, masked their presence completely, allowing them to slip through the shadows undetected. The next morning, Gati and Dati eagerly set out on their adventure, with Gati listening intently to the wind's every whisper while Dati stood by ready to follow their lead. The excitement was palpable as they took their first steps toward freedom, each heartbeat quickening with the anticipation of what lay ahead. Their determination and resourcefulness would be put to the ultimate test as they embarked on this perilous journey to reclaim their liberty.

Determined to free their people from the tyrannical rule of the Hagi, Gati and Dati launched a guerrilla war campaign. They rallied a fierce army of warriors, honing their skills in wrestling and martial arts. With unwavering discipline and patience, they instilled in their warriors the values of calmness and respect as the keys to victory. Gati rose as the formidable leader of the army, while Dati served as the wise adviser and head of training. Together, they meticulously planned their assault on the Fahi kingdom, which was under the oppressive rule of King Sempe. They struck swiftly, first conquering Giha and liberating the jungle prison with the miraculous liquid from the tree. As they prepared to face the Hagi forces in the Fahi Kingdom, Gati, Dati, and their unseen army were unstoppable. Their invisible presence confounded their enemies, allowing them to swiftly overtake Giha and advance toward their ultimate target. With a blink of an eye, they triumphantly seized control of the Fahi Kingdom in the exhilarating climax of their daring campaign.

Hagi and their chief were in a state of confusion, and things escalated into a fierce battle among themselves. Despite their defeat, they managed to escape into the jungle forest, fleeing from the invisible warriors. Meanwhile, Gati reclaimed his forefather's kingdom and ascended to the throne as the new king of the Fahi Kingdom. His reign was marked by kindness and respect toward his followers. The Talking Wind, a mystical presence, remained in the Fahi Kingdom, guiding King Gati on the path to success. Under Gati's rule, the Fahi Kingdom flourished once again, becoming a formidable superpower. Eventually, the Talking Wind expressed its desire to depart and aid other kingdoms in need. Gati was saddened by the departure of his best friend and advisor, but he knew it was for the greater good. Early one Sunday morning, as some were still lost in dreams, the Talking Wind bid farewell to the Fahi Kingdom and its beloved friend.

As the Talking Wind continued on its journey, King Gati could still faintly hear the voice slowly fading away in the distance. The people of the Fahi Kingdom had gathered together to bid a heartfelt farewell to their unseen hero, waving and shouting their appreciation to the mystical wind. Suddenly, a miraculous downpour of rain began, a much-needed gift from the wind that had not graced the kingdom since the passing of Chief Tiga. King Gati, overwhelmed with gratitude, exclaimed to the wind, "I will forever cherish your guidance and wisdom!" Two years later, King Gati found love and married Queen Nagi, and the couple was blessed with a beautiful son named Gatiti. Dati, loyal to the Fahi Kingdom, continued to serve as a warrior and army trainer, pledging an oath to the Orth to protect Chief Gati and safeguard the kingdom for generations to come.

THE END

CHIEF GATITI AND THE RETURN OF THE TALKING WIND

(Part 2)

Once upon a time, Chief Gati emerged victorious in the epic war against Chief Sempe of the Hagi! He became the revered and peaceful king of the Fahi Kingdom, leading his kingdom to greatness. The Fahi Kingdom thrived as the most advanced of all the kingdoms, flourishing on its incredibly fertile soil. Gati, known as the son of the wind, teamed up with Dati to revolutionize the kingdom's army with innovative war strategies. Sadly, Dati passed away, but his legacy of independence lives on in the Fahi Kingdom. Just before his passing, Dati and his wife, Kaji, were blessed with a son named Pago, who inherited his father's remarkable warrior skills. Chief Gati and Queen Nagi also welcomed a son named Gatiti, who was adored by his father. Despite their hopes for more children, Nagi faced numerous heartbreaking miscarriages. Gatiti lived a humble life, embodying the true qualities of a royal prince.

Gatiti was diligently trained by the warriors every single day of the week, immersing himself in the company of Pago and the orphaned children within the enchanting walls of Fahi Kingdom. The bond between Gatiti and Pago was as strong as that of their fathers, solidified through shared experiences and unwavering loyalty. However, tragedy struck the peaceful kingdom on a somber Sunday morning as a fierce storm unleashed its wrath, causing widespread flooding and destruction. The revered Chief Gati, who had recently celebrated his three hundred and ninetieth birthday, succumbed to the forces of nature, leaving behind a grieving Queen Nagi, a devastated Gatiti, and a mourning kingdom. As Chief Gati peacefully passed from this world to the next, reuniting with his departed friend Dati, the Fahi Kingdom honored his memory with a monthlong celebration of his extraordinary life, marked by peace, reverence, and everlasting love.

Gatiti, the only son, was joyously crowned as the new Chief of the Fahi Kingdom! Just like his father, Chief Gati, Gatiti was adored by the people of Fahi. Excitingly, Gatiti chose Pago as his adviser despite their similar ages. Pago was appointed as the chief adviser, along with the wise elders of the Kingdom. However, there were treacherous individuals in the kingdom, with Jatu being one of them. Jatu, a mixed child with a Hagi father and a Fahi mother, held a deep-seated grudge against Chief Gati and his son Gatiti. Influenced by the spirit of Chief Sempe, a Hagi commander who had disappeared into the jungle prison, Jatu was determined to rebel against the Fahi Kingdom. Chief Gatiti had transformed the jungle prison into a flourishing forest for hunting and gathering firewood while the Fahi villagers frequented the area for herbs and fruits. Jatu's mind was consumed by visions of Sempe, urging him to conduct rituals at the sacred tree in exchange for unimaginable wealth and power. Jatu was willing to go to any lengths to resurrect Chief Sempe and the mighty Hagi warriors!

At the stroke of midnight, Jatu daringly slipped out of the kingdom's confines and ventured into the depths of the jungle forest. With unwavering determination, Jatu knelt before the ancient miracle tree and began the sacred rituals to summon Sempe back from the realm of the lost. As the incantations reached their peak, a fierce thunderstorm erupted over the Fahi Kingdom, accompanied by a dazzling flash of lightning. From within the heart of the miracle tree emerged Chief Sempe and his fierce Hagi warriors, heralding their triumphant return from the shadows. In a swift and bold move, Chief Sempe of the Hagi warriors obliterated Jatu from existence, sending a chill down Chief Gatiti's spine as he awoke in horror. The ominous sight of monstrous bats blotting out the skies forewarned of the impending doom that awaited the Fahi Kingdom. Turning their gaze to the eastern horizon, Sempe and his monstrous warriors embarked on a relentless campaign of conquest, overpowering Chief Gatiti and his dwindling forces. In the aftermath of their defeat, Chief Gatiti and Pago fled westward into the neighboring Gahi Kingdom, leaving behind a path of destruction and sorrow. The once-mighty Fahi Kingdom succumbed to the merciless rule of Chief Sempe and his marauding Hagi warriors, with the Queen and her subjects falling victim to the ravages of war. With each successive invasion, the lands descended into chaos, lives were lost, and countless souls were left displaced and destitute in the wake of the relentless onslaught.

Gatiti and Pago, along with a small group of warriors, fled to the far west of the Gahi Kingdom in order to escape the pursuing Hagi monsters. Despite the danger, Gatiti bravely instructed Pago to lead a mission to rescue Queen Cabima, who tragically lost her life during the rescue attempt. Upon Pago's return to the Giha Kingdom, he appeared visibly shaken and fearful, prompting Gatiti to call out for help from his father. The Talking Wind, a mystical entity that had once aided their people, responded in a gentle voice, bringing some comfort to Gatiti in the midst of sorrow. With his warriors gone, Gatiti turned to Pago, his trusted advisor, for assistance. Together, they sought help from Chief Gihaha of the Giha Kingdom, who generously provided thirty warriors. To their amazement, the Talking Wind used its magic to multiply the warriors into two groups, creating a powerful force resembling twin brothers.

Gatiti and Pago, the leaders of their tribe, meticulously trained their warriors in a wide range of skills, from combat techniques to martial arts, wrestling, and even long-distance running. Chief Sempe exuded unwavering confidence, to the extent that he believed Gatiti had met his demise. When Gatiti's spies encountered obstacles in the tightly secured Fahi Kingdom, a cunning plan was hatched. The Talking Wind, assuming the guise of a beguiling woman named

Mahi, was tasked with a critical mission. Mahi captivated Chief Sempe at a clandestine gathering with her mesmerizing dance and entertainment. Upon exiting the party, Mahi shed her disguise and revealed the exact location of Chief Sempe's fortress to Gatiti, Pago, and herself. With this crucial information, they swiftly devised a strategic plan to mount a decisive attack on the unsuspecting Fahi Kingdom.

After sunset, the double warriors eagerly drank the water given to them by Chief Gatiti and the Talking Wind. Their minds were instantly sharpened, and they could now hear the whispers of the wind. It was unbelievable! The sixty warriors roared with determination, ready to conquer. And on the day of the attack, a powerful wind blew—the Talking Wind in action. With their newfound clarity, Gatiti, Pago, and the double warriors were guided on the path to victory. They stormed the kingdom, and before they knew it, Chief Sempe was captured, though he met his demise in his futile resistance. The battle was swift, lasting no more than three hours, and Fahi was reclaimed from the clutches of the tyrant. Thanks to the advice of the Talking Wind, Chief Gatiti gave water from the miracle tree to the Hagi warriors. And just like that, they transformed into formidable soldiers once again, bringing prosperity back to the Fahi Kingdom! The story of the brave warriors who defeated the tyrant Chief Sempe spread far and wide, inspiring other kingdoms to stand up against oppression.

Chief Gatiti was hailed as a hero, his leadership skills and wisdom praised by all. The Talking Wind continued to guide the people of Fahi, ensuring peace and prosperity for generations to come. After the glorious victory, the light burst back into Fahi Kingdom, flooding the land with pure joy and boundless hope! The people of Fahi Kingdom erupted in jubilant cheers, filling the air with the sounds of joyous dancing, triumphant singing, and wild celebration! Chief Gatiti, overflowing with gratitude, was exalted as the eighth Chief of Fahi Kingdom, a true beacon of strength and unity! Pago, the fearless and skilled warrior, proudly stepped into his father Dati's mighty shoes as the head of the army, poised to lead his people into a bright new era of peace and prosperity! The Talking Wind, a mystical presence that had bestowed guidance and wisdom upon Fahi Kingdom, chose to stay for eternity, a powerful testament to the profound bond formed with the people. Chief Gatiti, recognizing the invaluable role of the Talking Wind, bestowed upon her the honorary name Sakima, meaning "The Peace Fighter," a title that honored her unwavering commitment to safeguarding the kingdom.

As Chief Gatiti poured out his heartfelt thanks to Sakima, a dazzling white light burst forth from the wind, enveloping him in a radiant glow that symbolized the unbreakable bond between them. Sakima's spirit, now intertwined with Chief Gatiti's, would forever stand guard over and protect Fahi Kingdom from any looming threat. Long live Chief Gatiti, Pago, the double warriors, Sakima, and the indomitable spirit of Fahi Kingdom, united in unyielding strength and harmonious unity for countless generations to come!

THE END

DUKA VILLAGE, MAWIKO, AND THE GREEN PEOPLE

(Part 1)

Once upon a time, nestled within the lush landscape of Duka Village, there stood a dazzling, enchanting, and extraordinary community that shone as the grandest in all the land! Duka was not just any village—it was a vibrant tapestry woven from the threads of three incredible tribes: the Ndaga, Gaso, and Leko. Among them, the Ndaga tribe reigned as the largest, led by the remarkable Chief Mako, a figure who transcended mere leadership to embody the very essence of heroism. Chief Mako's presence was a beacon of light and hope, his kindness, generosity, and compassion radiating like a warm embrace that touched the hearts of all his villagers and tribespeople. His dedication to fostering harmony and unity among the tribes was unwavering, and he tirelessly worked to ensure that every soul in Duka felt valued and cherished. Chief Mako's wisdom and fairness were legendary. His reputation as a fair and caring leader spread far and wide, earning him the love and respect of not just his own village but of all the neighboring communities as well. In every action he took, Chief Mako embodied the spirit of selflessness and service, making him a true guardian of peace and prosperity in Duka Village.

The unity among the tribes of Duka Village was a testament to Chief Mako's leadership, as he tirelessly mediated disputes and encouraged collaboration among the Ndaga, Gaso, and Leko. His ability to listen attentively and empathize with others made him a beloved figure not only within his own community but also in the surrounding villages. Chief Mako's reputation for fairness and justice was unmatched, as he always sought to make decisions that bene-fitted the greater good of all tribes. His commitment to upholding peace and harmony in Duka Village was unwavering, and his actions inspired others to follow in his footsteps. Chief Mako's legacy as a compassionate and selfless leader continued to grow, with stories of his deeds spreading far and wide, becoming a source of inspiration for all who heard them. The impact of Chief Mako's leadership extended beyond the borders of Duka Village, earning him a place of honor and respect among all who knew of his legendary deeds.

One of Duka Village's most prominent source of livelihood was fishing, mainly because there were two large and plentiful lakes that lay within its borders. The lakes were known to the villagers as Tima and Bati, and every day many villagers could be seen fishing along their shores. Aside from some small-scale farming, traditional farm-ing practices were less common in Duka Village due to the infer-tile soil and years of drought that plagued the area. In addition to fishing, Duka villagers engaged in barter trade and exchanged fish with neighboring villages, as well as importing food from neighbor-ing Damu Village. Duka Village was known for being a community of kind and welcoming people, always open to visitors who wished to work and share their skills. Furthermore, Duka villagers were very spiritual and worshipped Mawiko, the god of peace, harmony, and safety.

The villagers of Duka were skilled craftspeople, known for their intricate wood carvings and colorful textiles that were highly sought after in the neighboring villages. They also had a rich tradition of sto-rytelling, passing down tales of their ancestors and the history of their village through generations. The community of Duka was tightly knit, with strong bonds of kinship and mutual support that ensured everyone was cared for in times of need. The village was also known for its vibrant festivals and celebrations, where music, dance, and feasting brought the community together in joy and unity. Overall, Duka Village was a place of resilience, creativity, and a deep cultural heritage that was cherished by all who called it home.

Chief Mako, revered as the head of spirituality in Duka Village, possessed a unique ability to channel the spirits of ancestors during worship, offering glimpses into the future that were crucial for the survival of the community. Villagers often turned to Chief Mako in times of need and adversity, seeking his guidance and wisdom to navigate through challenges. His prophetic visions, both desired and unwelcome, were believed to always come to fruition, shaping the destiny of the village. Alongside Chief Mako, the villagers worshipped Mawiko, their god of peace and harmony, whom they honored with monthly sacrifices. Once a year, the village engaged in a spirited game of rope pulling to determine the strongest individuals, who were then recruited into the esteemed Duka army to safeguard their home and chief. The villagers took immense pride in their village and its grandeur, cherishing the traditions and values that bound them together.

It all happened during the year of the lunar eclipse when most villagers noticed the water levels in the neighboring lakes starting to rise! And let me tell you, it was a sight to behold! At first, the floods were just a minor annoyance causing some damage to homes and shacks near the lakes. But then, the water didn't recede as usual—it just stayed there! Can you imagine the fear and panic that struck the hearts of the villagers? Especially those who depended on the lake for their livelihood! They were being forced to leave their homes and start anew. The people of Duka Village even began offering regular sacrifices to Mawiko, going as far as sacrificing perfectly healthy cows and goats! But the troubles didn't stop there—some villagers started falling ill with mysterious sicknesses, which others believed were curses from jealous neighbors! The situation in Duka Village grew increasingly dire as time went on! Some believed that Mawiko was punishing them because outsiders from different tribes had disrespected the village's traditions. This only fueled more tension and conflict among the villagers! The village was in turmoil!

Duka Village had faced its share of hardships before, but never to the extent of such consistent flooding and the spread of what seemed like an incurable disease that led to severe vomiting, diarrhea, and coughing! At first, the villagers thought both would eventually fade away like other illnesses and natural disasters before this, and that the village was just under a curse. But everyone soon realized that this could not be the doings of just a curse. Every day, more and more Duka villagers died, and families began to perish completely, wiping out an entire generation! Those most affected were the fishermen and villagers living on the shores of Lake Tima and Lake Bati, causing a direct impact on all commercial activities in the village. As the disease remained, villagers who fell ill were discriminated against and shunned in the community. With time, villagers began running away from Duka to find better lives in other villages, and this migration soon caused the spread of the curse to Fahi Village and its neighbors!

The situation became dire as resources dwindled and hope seemed to fade away, leaving behind a once vibrant village on the brink of collapse. The sense of despair and desperation hung heavy in the air as the villagers struggled to find a solution to the seemingly unstoppable curse that had befallen their home. Despite their best efforts, the disease continued to ravage the community, leaving behind a trail of devastation and heartbreak. The once bustling streets of Duka now lay empty and desolate, a haunting reminder of the tragedy that had befallen the village. But amid the darkness, a glimmer of hope emerged as a group of brave villagers banded together to fight against the curse, determined to reclaim their once-thriving community and restore peace and prosperity to their beloved home.

Amid the chaos of death, Chief Mako roared for Mawiko to descend and rescue his people! The flood ceased, bringing immense relief and jubilation to the resilient villagers. But Chief Mako's desperate pleas were only partially answered. The deadly disease persisted, snuffing out lives of all ages and leaving devastation in its wake. With unwavering determination, the villagers crafted a powerful poem:

Mawiko save us from the curse,

it is killing our beloved ones,

it is killing young ones and old ones,

We cannot hide from it. It is killing the rich and the poor,

It is emptying houses and destroying generations,

The weak ones and warriors are dying from the curse.

It kills people during the day and night,

it also kills at sunrise and sunset,

it kills when raining and cloudy,

please use your powers to save us from the curse,

Mawiko,

we have cried to the maximum,

what can we do to stop this curse,

Please save us from the curse.

Fathers, mothers, grandparents, sons, and daughters kept dying! Duka villagers were filled with uncertainty, wondering if life would ever return to normal.

Chief Mako, a man known for having four wives in a polygamous marriage, tragically succumbed to the disease that had already claimed the lives of two of his wives. Despite seeking forgiveness from Mawiko, he too fell ill and eventually passed away, facing a fate that remained unchanged. Chief Mako's son, Makoko, took power upon the death of his father, becoming the fifth Chief of Duka Village and the only chief to take power in such dark times when Duka Village was full of suffering, misery, and fear. Much to the villagers' surprise, Chief Makoko was a great leader; he was not only well-educated and a philosopher, but also a great problem solver. Soon after taking power, he began accepting foreigners into his village and supported modernization. He believed this might be a solution to the so-called curse and the loss of so many lives and generations. During this time, Chief Makoko heard about the Green People, who lived far east of Duka Village. In an eloquently written letter, he requested the Green People to come to Duka Village and investigate the curse, as they were known for their understanding of illnesses and the science of the body.

The Green People, who had already integrated themselves into civilization for numerous decades, possessed an unparalleled level of expertise in illnesses and the intricacies of the human body, all thanks to their groundbreaking advancements in science and technology! Upon their arrival in the humble Duka Village, the villagers were met with a mix of fear and astonishment at the sight of these towering beings with their striking reddish-green hair and formidable weaponry. The Green People's pragmatic philosophies and profound comprehension of human anatomy left the Duka villagers utterly mesmerized. Such was the extent of their reverence for science, technology, and pragmatic reasoning that they even disregarded Mawiko, the revered god of the Duka, as their own beliefs held far greater sway over their minds and hearts!

Upon their arrival, Chief Makoko eagerly shared the entire story with the Green People, detailing the origins of the curse from Mawiko. As he spoke, the Green People exchanged glances, nodding, and pulling faces in understanding and agreement. Once Chief Makoko finished recounting the events of the past few months, a representative from the Green People tribe stood up to address the group. She enthusiastically clarified that the unfolding events were not due to a curse but rather a widespread epidemic known as Limu. This disease had plagued their community for years, claiming the lives of many. The Green People outlined how the disease spread, how it could be controlled, and shared measures to reduce the death toll in Duka Village. Their knowledge and willingness to help filled Chief Makoko with hope for the future. The chief was relieved to learn the true cause of the affliction and was grateful for the Green People's expertise in combating the epidemic. He felt a sense of unity and collaboration between the tribes, leading him to believe that together they could overcome any challenges that lay ahead.

The Green People were incredibly passionate about supporting the Duka Village! They dedicated a significant amount of time to initiate community workshops focused on disease prevention. Their approach to teaching was straightforward, as they believed that understanding the scientific aspects of health could not only benefit the body but also the spirit. The villagers were astounded to learn that engaging in multiple partners and unprotected sexual activity were significant contributors to Limu. The Green People imparted invaluable knowledge on the best practices to minimize the transmission of the disease, such as practicing abstinence, avoiding the sharing of sharp objects, maintaining fidelity to one partner, and using condoms when necessary. They even provided condoms and tools for detecting Limu in blood samples! Chief Makoko, who had warmly welcomed the Green People, courageously volunteered to be the first to undergo testing. The news of his negative test result brought immense relief and joy to the entire village. The positive impact of their efforts was truly remarkable!

Chief Makoko was overjoyed to see a significant turnout of villagers willing to be tested for Limu. The Green People promptly offered consultation and medication to those who tested positive, while those who tested negative were invited to a follow-up workshop. The workshop focused on the importance of safe sex practices, partner status awareness, and overcoming stigma and discrimination by treating others with dignity and respect. It was not surprising that the majority of Duka villagers heeded the advice of the Green People, as the threat of Limu had the potential to devastate the entire village.

After five long years of dedication and perseverance by the amazing Green People, the Duka Village population started to soar, and a wave of progress and development swept through the community. Despite the ongoing challenge of Lima disease, the village saw a resurgence in commercial activities. The Green People continued their tireless efforts to find a cure and improve treatment methods. Thanks to their unwavering support, the health sector in Duka Village has been revolutionized, with more and more people thriving. The community rallied together to support the Green People's mission, working side by side to enhance the overall quality of life in the village. With upgraded infrastructure and enhanced healthcare access, Duka Village overcame numerous obstacles. The Green People's unwavering dedication and commitment ignited a sense of hope and unity among the residents, paving the way for a brighter future for everyone.

THE END

WAR IN DUKA VILLAGE

(Part 2)

Once upon a time, Duka Village was the most thriving and vibrant community in the west, with a population that was rapidly expanding! It boasted top-notch infrastructure and social services that were dedicated to the health and well-being of all its residents, including well-maintained roads, state-of-the-art hospitals, and top-notch schools. Duka was home to four unique tribes—the Ndaga, Gaso, Leko, and the Green People. The Green People followed their spiritual leader, Gandi, and worked hand in hand with the beloved Chief of Duka, Chief Makoko, in a bond of friendship and brotherhood. What's more, all four tribes spoke the same language, Buka, making communication seamless and easy among all groups. To top it all off, a protective wall surrounding Duka Village, built by the villagers themselves, is a powerful display of unity. And despite its already impressive status, new faces from neighboring villages were constantly flocking to Duka Village in search of a brighter future, a better education, and improved healthcare services. The excitement in the air was palpable as Duka continued to grow and thrive!

In Duka Village, the Green People were not only known for their innovation and wealth of knowledge but also for their significant contribution to the structural modernization and development of the village. Decades earlier, when they chose to settle in Duka Village, the Green People embarked on a mission to transform the living conditions of the villagers. They dedicated their time and resources to reconstructing residential homes, replacing the traditional grass-thatched housing with more modernized structures that had tin roofs. These new homes provided better protection for families against the natural elements, reducing the risk of fires that had previously destroyed homes and lives in the village. Despite their efforts in improving the physical infrastructure of the village, the Green People also shared their expertise in health and well-being with the villagers. However, despite their best efforts, the prevalence of Limu continued to rise in Duka Village, causing great alarm and concern among the community members.

Mawiko, the almighty god revered by all the villagers of Duka, was held in high esteem, while Kaga was specifically worshipped by the Green People living in the vibrant west side of the village. The Mawiko shrine stood proudly on the east side, a symbol of power and tradition, while the Kaga shrine was a place of reverence and connection to nature. Sati, the esteemed keeper of the Mawiko shrine, was a descendant of the powerful ruling family of Duka, with a lineage that stretched back generations. And let's not forget Chief Makoko, the long-reigning leader of the village and older brother to Sati, son of the great Chief Mako who had ruled before him. For a decade now, Sati has harbored a burning desire to claim the title of chief for himself, believing he was more deserving than his younger brother. His resentment simmered in silence, festering and growing stronger with each passing year, until it boiled over into a series of failed attempts to overthrow Chief Makoko and claim the title for himself. But Sati's thirst for power reached its peak when he hatched a devious plot to sow discord between Chief Makoko and the Green People, knowing it would sow distrust and chaos throughout the entire village, threatening the very fabric of their society.

On a dark stormy night, Sati jolted awake at midnight in the pitch-black, his mind consumed by a sinister plan. With a heart pounding with excitement and a twisted sense of purpose, he stealthily made his way to the west side of Duka Village, daring to trespass into the Green People's land under the cover of darkness. Ignited by a dangerous combination of rage and greed, he set ablaze their sacred shrine, leaving a piece of cloth from the royal family as a twisted calling card, a symbol of his malevolent intentions. With adrenaline coursing through his veins, he swiftly escaped back to the east side, his devious plan unfolding with each step he took in the shadows of the night. But Sati's thirst for destruction was far from quenched; his soul was consumed by chaos, and there was no room for calm within him. In a fit of jealousy and fury, he made his way to Mawiko's shrine. His eyes filled with a maniacal grin as he set it alight, reveling in the destruction he had caused. As the flames danced in the night, casting an eerie glow on his twisted features, Sati's descent into darkness seemed inevitable, his actions driven by a darkness that seemed to consume his very being.

When news of the dual fires spread through the village, chaos ensued as villagers and royal leaders alike were left reeling from the devastating loss of their cherished shrines. The once peaceful east and west villages were now consumed with anguish and despair, while Duka Village became a hub of fear and uncertainty. Questions swirled through the air as everyone pondered who could have orchestrated such a destructive event. As Chief Makoko, the royal family, and the village elders gathered to address the situation, the Green People began their own investigation, uncovering a crucial clue—the royal family's cloth amid the wreckage. This discovery only fueled their suspicions, leading them to believe that the royal family was behind the destruction at the Kaga shrine. In response, the royal family quickly pointed fingers at the Green People, accusing them of being responsible for the devastation of their shrine. The tension between the two groups continued to escalate, deepening the mystery and complexity of the situation. With each new development, the plot thickened, leaving both sides embroiled in a web of accusations and uncertainty.

Sita was ecstatically gleeful because his cunning plan had succeeded beyond his wildest dreams! The village was now split into two opposing sides, causing chaos and pain throughout. The original

Duka people rallied behind Chief Makoko, while the Green People stood united under their spiritual leader, Gandi. The thirst for revenge was palpable, driving both sides to prepare for war with unmatched determination. The drums of war were beating louder and louder, and soon, Duka Village would be plunged into a battle unlike any other. Chief Makoko's tribes trained relentlessly, while Gandi's Green People matched their every move, ready to defend their beliefs at any cost. The tension in the air was thick with anticipation as the looming battle cast a shadow over the once-peaceful village. The sound of weapons being sharpened and armor being donned echoed through the streets, a grim reminder of the impending conflict that would tear the community apart. Each side hardened their resolve, knowing that the fate of their people rested on the outcome of the upcoming clash. As the sun set on the horizon, the atmosphere was charged with a mix of fear, anticipation, and a fierce determination to emerge victorious in the battle that lay ahead.

Throughout history, it has been widely documented that the villagers of Duka were renowned for their expertise in crafting a unique weapon known as the Gahabo. This weapon, resembling a spear with three piercing points, held a deadly secret—the tips were infused with venom extracted from the Kene, a serpentlike creature found in the forests surrounding Duka. Kene's venom was so potent that even a slight touch could prove fatal. In stark contrast, the inhabitants of the Green People wielded a weapon known as Hada. This firearm, constructed from a blend of iron and copper, fires small copper bullets with such force that the sound of a single shot reverberated throughout the nearby canyons. The Hada was considered a groundbreaking innovation and was hailed as the most advanced and lethal weapon of its era.

When the battle between Duka Village and the Green People finally broke out, causing many villagers to flee in search of safety and peace, Chief Makoko's heart was heavy with fear for his people and their crops. On the second day of the conflict, Chief Makoko had a vivid dream where Mawiko, the village guardian spirit, appeared to him. Mawiko instructed Chief Makoko to use the water from the swamp on the west side, near the demolished shrine, for protection.

According to Mawiko, this water had the power to act as a shield against any weaponry. In his dream, Mawiko explained how to use the water—by rubbing it all over the body, especially on the warriors who would be entering the battle. When Chief Makoko woke from his slumber, he wasted no time in following Mawiko's instructions.

The next day, just before sunrise, Chief Makoko collected buckets of swamp water, a ritual he believed would protect his fighters in battle. Instructing his warriors to smear the water on their bodies, he also urged them to send their loved ones to collect more water for added protection. The Duka warriors even went as far as putting yam stems in their ears to block out the noise of the battle. As the battle raged on, the Duka people, led by Chief Makoko, emerged victorious on the second day. Chief Makoko marveled at the power of the swamp water, which seemed to act as a shield against the Green People's weaponry. Each bullet that was fired seemed to be deflected by the mystical properties of the swamp water, proving to be a crucial element in their triumph.

Gandi, overwhelmed by the devastation brought about by the war, made his way back to the ruined shrine with a heavy heart, contemplating how such a conflict had escalated to such destructive heights. As he walked through the remnants of the shrine under the soft glow of the moonlight, a glint caught his eye amid the ashes. Upon closer inspection, he realized he had stumbled upon a significant discovery—none other than Sita's royal ring. Puzzled by how it could have ended up there, Gandi considered the possibilities. Had it slipped off during the chaos of the battle, or had it been lost before the shrine was engulfed in flames? Determined to uncover the truth, Gandi wasted no time in dispatching a messenger to Chief Makoko with the mysterious find.

Within hours, Gandi and Chief Makoko excitedly met to discuss everything in detail. They delved into every aspect of the situation, analyzing every possible angle. As soon as they finished talking, Chief Makoko eagerly called for a royal meeting to address the pressing issue at hand. The tension in the room was palpable as Sita was questioned about his royal ring being found in the Kaga shrine. His facade of composure quickly crumbled, his face turning ashen with fear. The fear in his eyes was unmistakable, sending a chill down everyone's spine. To everyone's shock, Sita attempted to defend himself, his voice shaky as he denied any knowledge of how his royal ring ended up in the ashes at the Kaga shrine. The atmosphere in the room grew even more tense as accusations flew and suspicions mounted.

After much deliberation and internal struggle, Chief Makoko ultimately made the difficult decision to place Sita in the revered cultural court. This court, steeped in tradition and history, had been a cornerstone of the Duka Village for generations. Located in a small mystical shrine just north of the village, the cultural court held immense power in the eyes of the villagers. The fate of those on trial was believed to be determined by the mystical powers of the shrine and the collective judgment of the community. Those who entered the shrine and emerged unscathed were deemed innocent and could walk free. However, those found guilty met a swift and irreversible demise within the shrine's walls. Sita, overwhelmed with fear and dread, knew that his chances of survival were slim. His guilt was written all over his face, a palpable aura of shame and remorse surrounding him. As the eyes of the villagers bore into him, Sita felt the weight of impending doom pressing down on him. Unable to bear the tension any longer, Sita broke down and confessed to his crimes, the truth pouring out of him uncontrollably like a floodgate that had been opened. The truth, raw and unfiltered, laid bare the depths of Sita's wrongdoing, leaving no room for doubt or denial.

He narrated the entire crime in front of Chief Makoko, Gandi, and Duka villagers, causing a moment of surprise and pure silence to fall over the crowd. The details of his heinous act sent shivers down the spines of those listening, leaving them in disbelief at the evil that had transpired in their peaceful village. After finishing, Sita was overwhelmed with fear and could only think of one thing—to escape from the village as quickly as possible. The weight of his guilt and the impending consequences of his actions loomed over him like a dark cloud, driving him to desperation. Tragically, as he attempted to flee, he was struck down by a bolt of lightning—a sudden and merciless end to his life. Mawiko and Kaga, filled with anger and hunger for justice, decided to punish Sita in a way that mirrored the severity of his actions and the death toll from the two days of war.

After the tragic death of Sati due to lightning, Chief Makoko and Gandi showed great humility by offering sincere apologies to the Green People and all Duka Villagers. In a gesture of goodwill, Chief Makoko generously granted land to the Green People, paving the way for the resolution of misunderstandings and the beginning of the reconstruction of the ravaged buildings. The villagers were not only compensated for their losses but also witnessed the restoration of the sacred Kaga and Mawiko shrines through the collaborative efforts of both sides. Furthermore, an army of skilled warriors was assembled to safeguard Duka Village from any potential external threats, ensuring the safety and security of all residents.

Today, Duka Village stands as a shining example of progress and development, a testament to the successful partnership between Duka villagers and the Green People. Gandi's presence among the members of the royal family council serves as a powerful symbol of unity and peace, reflecting the harmonious coexistence that has been achieved through mutual understanding and cooperation. Let us raise our glasses in celebration of Chief Makoko and the thriving community of Duka Village, as they continue to flourish and prosper in ways that were once unimaginable!

THE END

GAMU VILLAGE

Once upon a time, in a village called Gamu, there was a beloved leader named Gandu. Gandu was a kind and wise chief who always looked out for his villagers. Gamu Village was truly stunning, with a mix of equatorial and tropical climates, making it a special place to live. The village would often receive heavy rains accompanied by the rumble of thunder, making it feel cozy and alive. One of the highlights of Gamu Village was the gorgeous river called Razo, flowing gracefully through the land. On the southern side, there was a swamp with a small lake where the animals would gather to swim and play games like hide and sink. The frogs, especially Tila, loved to visit the swamp in the evenings to dance and sing their hearts out. Tila's favorite tune was *ngonga, ngonge, ngongi*, to which the snakes (Sota) would playfully respond with *nsa, nse, nsi*. The other animals would relax under the stars, gazing up at the beautiful sky. Life in Gamu Village revolved around fishing and farming, with fish, potatoes, and seasonal White Ants being the main products sold at the weekly market on Fridays. The bustling Gamu Village market would come alive, with White Ants flying off the shelves as the Sotas eagerly stocked up on their favorite treat. It was a sight to behold—a true celebration of life in the vibrant village of Gamu!

The incredible citizen, Kamu, resided in the vibrant Gamu Village! Kamu, the village timekeeper, was none other than a wise old rooster who was proudly born and raised in Gamu Village. Every morning, Kamu diligently rose early to awaken all the animals, ensuring they were ready to embark on their daily adventures. But one fateful day, the daring Sota banded together and launched a rebellion, invading the peaceful Gamu Village. Their target? None other than the beloved Chief Gandu and his loyal followers. The root of Sota's rebellion? Their insatiable hunger for control over the coveted seasonal White Ants collected by all the animals in Gamu Village. As the battle ensued, Sota emerged victorious, causing Chief Gandu and his supporters to flee in fear, seeking refuge in neighboring villages. The cunning snakes of Sota swiftly claimed dominion over Gamu Village, bringing their kin and allies along for the ride. They boldly seized ownership of all the once-shared properties and resources, leaving the village forever changed.

The Gamu villagers who chose to stay were incredibly mistreated and denied their rights, but things were about to get exciting! Sota had a strong affection for White Ants and implemented a strict law prohibiting other animals from eating them. Deliveries were scheduled every Friday morning before the village market, all for Lenko, the new chief. Lenko's leadership was harsh, showing favoritism toward Sota and treating others poorly. Sota didn't seem to care about the villagers or the environment, encouraging deforestation. Trade issues with neighboring villages made things worse. Deforestation continued as timber was exchanged for White Ants. Sota even started extracting sand from the river Razo, harming the ecosystem and causing the death of the Nyanja fish. Swamps turned into slums, where the less fortunate villagers lived. Despite the hardships, the villagers remained hopeful for a savior. Sota kept a close eye on the village, punishing those who opposed him. The village was full of drama and chaos, but the villagers were eagerly anticipating a change for the better!

Gamu villagers were living in constant fear; the suffering of animals in and around the village had reached a breaking point. They banded together in secret, desperate for a savior to come to their rescue. Goni (dragonfly), the fastest and most reliable villager, flew to Jagu Village to deliver a letter to Gandu, who had become a fisherman. Upon receiving the distressing letter, his heart broke at the state of his beloved Gamu Village. Determined to make a change, Chief Gandu gathered all the animals in need and formed a resistance against the oppressive Sota. Among the Sota was a noble snake named Muba, who secretly worked as a double agent for Gandu, bravely risking his life to provide valuable information. Armed with Muba's intel and weeks of intense training, Gandu and the resistance prepared to take on the Sota. But before the attack, they enlisted Muba's help to set a clever trap using White Ants, the Sota's favorite delicacy. The excitement and anticipation were palpable as they geared up for the ultimate showdown in Gamu Village. Victory was within reach, and the animals were ready to fight for their freedom!

At midnight, while everyone in Gamu Village was fast asleep, Muba sneaked into the Gamu Village store and started moving baskets of White Ants to the north side of the village, near Jagu Village. Muba did an amazing job setting up a trap by spreading the White Ants and Nyango grass in a big circle. Nyango grass was a type of grass that caused itching when in contact with the skin, and it was dreaded by the people of Sota. They despised it so much that they would even dig it out of their village. The resistance needed a victory, so they had to bring Nyango grass from Jagu Village. After setting up the trap, Muba went to talk to Kamu. Muba shared the ideas behind Gandu's resistance and the upcoming war with Kamu, who was thrilled to hear about their beloved Chief Gandu.

Muba asked Kamu to wake up Sota and all the animals in the village before sunrise for the sake of victory. Kamu agreed and began singing his wake-up song at four in the morning, two hours before sunrise. Sota were the first to wake up, and Gandu and the resistance were prepared to start the war. Excitedly, as it was in the plan, Muba went to Lenko and shared the news about the White Ants on the north side of the village. Muba led Lenko into the trap, knowing that both Lenko and Sota had a weakness for White Ants and wouldn't consider the risks of the dark. Lenko ordered all Sota to head to the north side to collect the White Ants. Little did they know, they were walking right into Muba's trap!

Muba boldly led the group into the circle of death, with Lenko and Sota eagerly following behind. Lenko quickly instructed Sota and the other animals to collect the White Ants under the dazzling stars. With the trap set, Muba confidently knew the escape route even before Chief Gandu and the resistance animals could make a move on Gamu Village. As Lenko and Sota entered the circle, Muba triumphantly sounded the trumpet, signaling the start of the epic showdown. Chief Gandu and the resistance animals emerged with determination, armed with thorns and stones, encircling Sota, and chanting powerful resistance slogans. The animals of Gamu Village rallied behind Gandu, leading to the dramatic downfall of Chief Lenko and the mighty Sota empire that very night. Chief Lenko was ultimately captured, and in a desperate attempt to break free, Sota bravely ran into thorns and Nyango grass, enduring severe injuries in the process.

By morning, Gamu Village was once again under the rule of Chief Gandu and the animals—victorious and joyous! The day was filled with celebrations as the heavy rain poured down, washing away all the past misery and suffering of the animals in Gamu Village. A new era was dawning in Gamu Village, with properties and resources returning to their rightful owners. All the animals who had left for neighboring villages came back to bask in the restored glory of their home. Muba and Kamu were honored with top positions in the new leadership as Chief Gandu's trusted advisers. Chief Gandu wasted no time in launching a campaign of afforestation and protecting the remaining swamps in Gamu Village. Every animal in the village planted at least two trees to support this important cause. Gamu Village now stands as the most beautiful and thriving village in the land!

THE END

KING TIMA AND VEGA VILLAGE

(The Hero Bee)

Once upon a time, there was a village in the north called Vega, also known as the Dark Village. Vega Village was enveloped in darkness from dawn till dusk and from dusk till dawn. The Vega villagers possessed keener eyesight compared to the inhabitants of neighboring areas like Koti Village, which was situated in the south of Vega. Koti Village differed from Vega in terms of culture, village structure, and economic progress. Koti Village was renowned as the City of Light. Following a tragic incident that plunged Vega into darkness, many of its residents migrated to Koti Village. This catastrophic event transformed Vega from a light-filled village to one shrouded in darkness. The Yati resided in Koti Village and were infamous for their formidable stingers. Despite living in a vibrant community bathed in light, the Yati did not produce honey. Vega, too, was once a village illuminated by light until their leader, Chief Timama, perished in a battle against the Yati, who were vying for territorial supremacy.

Timama, the beloved Fifth Chief of Vega Village, passed away in the war but left behind his son, Tima, who was adored by his father. Tima, a name bestowed upon him by Chief Timama, grew up with love and care. After his father's death, Tima's anger shook Vega

Village to its core, causing darkness to descend upon the land. The hunt for Tima by the Yati only added to the chaos. But Tima found solace and companionship with his good samaritan, Neza, and his twin best friends, Gakafo and Dakila. Despite his royal lineage, Tima grew up as a humble and kind boy, soaking in the traditions of Vega. His escapades from school to play with the twins only added to his adventurous spirit, especially when he ventured into the yam garden and swam in the rainwater collected by the leaves. Tima's journey as a Prince of Vega was just beginning, filled with excitement and discovery.

For several weeks, Nema had been under the impression that Tima was attending school, only to discover that he was not attending school. Tima was classmate with Deti. Deti, a village girl hailing from the east side of Vega, was the daughter of a yam farmer named Hati. One day, as Deti was returning home for lunch, she caught sight of Tima swimming in her father's yam garden. Alarmed, she promptly informed Nema of Tima's actions. Nema wasted no time investigating the situation and found Tima in the act. Tima, the son of the late Chief Timama and the Prince of Vega village, was so frightened that he began to tremble. Nema escorted him to school to meet with the head teacher, who was unaware of Tima's prestigious background.

The head teacher provided invaluable guidance to Tima, who was visibly scared and shaking. The counseling session turned out to be a huge success, marking the start of Tima's incredible journey to success in architecture! Tima transformed into a focused student, forming strong bonds with his classmates. He worked tirelessly, always finishing his work on time and helping his peers. After years of dedication, Prince Tima aced his final exams, securing top honors and graduating with a degree in architecture. On graduation day, Nema shocked the whole community by revealing that she had been nurturing and educating the lost Prince of Vega Village. This revelation left everyone in awe, showcasing Tima's unwavering determination and perseverance in conquering his obstacles to achieve greatness.

At the young age of twenty-five, Tima had blossomed into a diligent and responsible man. His serious demeanor was well-known, with smiles being a rare occurrence. However, on the day of his graduation party—something genuinely magical happened! As he presented Nema with a token of appreciation, a radiant smile lit up his face, casting a brilliant light across the darkened village of Vega. The villagers were left speechless by this sudden burst of light, shielding their eyes from the long-lost sunlight that had finally returned after three decades of absence. It was an extraordinary day, filled with boundless joy and renewed hope as the once-shadowed village reveled in the warmth of the sun's rays once again.

The Yati and their soldiers all started to turn into ashes, a consequence of the return of the long-lost Prince of Vega! The people of Vega erupted into cheers, exclaiming, "The prince has returned!" The joyful news quickly spread far and wide, reaching every corner of the land as Prince Tima made his way back to the Vega palace to reunite with his family! The following day, Prince Tima was officially crowned as the Sixth Chief of Vega Village, succeeding his father, Chief Timama! King Tima wasted no time in educating his people on the art of architecture, assigning various roles and responsibilities to the villagers! The men were tasked with building homes and collecting nectar from the flowers of Vega Village, while the women remained at home, caring for their children! Under Prince Tima's reign, Vega Village flourished, becoming the first village to boastfully construct houses! As the days passed, Prince Tima's leadership skills continued to shine, guiding the villagers toward prosperity and unity. His vision for Vega Village included implementing sustainable farming practices and organizing cultural events to celebrate the rich history of their ancestors. The villagers, inspired by their new chief, worked tirelessly to improve their community, building stronger bonds and creating a sense of belonging that had not been felt in generations. With Prince Tima at the helm, Vega Village became a shining example of what can be achieved through hard work, cooperation, and dedication to a common goal.

The light that came back to Vega Village brought with it incredible miracles! All the followers of King Tima suddenly started producing honey, a magical substance that was essential for the village. Not only was honey used as food, but it also had incredible healing properties for the villagers. King Tima motivated everyone to grow flowers and crops to ensure an abundance of nectar. With heavy rainfall and fertile soil, Vega Village flourished with produce and beautiful flowers. It quickly became the most powerful village in the region, earning the title "The Honey Village." The villagers of Vega were renowned for their exceptional house construction skills. Even today, humans continue to learn from King Tima and his followers, gaining knowledge in organization, leadership, and construction. Honey remains a valuable resource for humans, providing energy, aiding in weight loss, and promoting healing. King Tima's legacy lives on, forever remembered in the history of Vega Village and the world. The miracle of honey continues to be celebrated as one of the greatest wonders to ever bless Vega Village and the world!

Humans and modernity are the number one cause of death of the Vega people. Modernity has come with bad practices of spraying crops and flowers with chemicals, which have had devastating effects on the environment and on King Tima's followers. It is time for us to come together and take action to fight against these harmful practices that are leading to the decline of bee populations. Let us prioritize afforestation efforts to maintain a green environment and preserve the habitats of bees. Education is key; we must teach future generations about the negative impacts of chemical spraying on crops and the importance of choosing organic farming practices. Additionally, we must work toward protecting our rivers and lakes from pollution to ensure a healthy ecosystem for all creatures, including King Tami and his followers. By making these changes, we can ensure the survival of bees and humans alike for generations to come. Let us strive to coexist harmoniously with nature so that both bees and humans can thrive together.

THE END

YUKYE AND THE STONES

Once upon a time, in the vibrant village of Tena, there thrived an extraordinary family whose livelihood depended on the thrilling art of hunting. The illustrious patriarch, Kyeyuyu, dwelled in a magnificent glass-thatched abode on the enchanting western outskirts of the village. Kyeyuyu, a man of great humility, was blissfully wed to the lovely Nagi, and their joyful union bore nine spirited children, including the remarkable Yukye. Renowned far and wide as the most skilled hunter in all of Tena, Kyeyuyu fearlessly ventured into the dense forest alongside his faithful companions, the loyal dogs Makyeya and Nadiwa, always returning triumphant with succulent meat wrapped in fragrant banana leaves.

Among his beloved offspring, Yukye, the bold and adventurous second-eldest son, shared his father's passion for hunting and was blessed with a touch of extraordinary luck. But beyond his prowess in the art of hunting, Yukye's heart belonged to the thrilling game of soccer, a sport that ignited a fiery passion deep within his soul. In addition to his hunting duties, Yukye took great care to ensure that Makyeya and Nadiwa were duly rewarded for their loyalty and bravery, roasting their delectable legs and tails as a token of gratitude. The devoted dogs, in turn, stood steadfast by the Kyeyuyu family, offering unwavering loyalty and protection. Amid his daily chores of fetching water from the village well, Yukye would often find joy in playfully kicking stones along the dusty path, all the while balancing a cumbersome ten-liter jerrican with ease, a habit that revealed his unwavering love for the beautiful game of soccer.

Yukye kicked them barefoot! His strong feet could kick them without even a scratch. The stones despised it, but they did nothing. Yukye and his siblings could not attend school because Kyeyuyu, a hunter, and Nagi, a stay-at-home mom, couldn't afford it. Their children stayed home to help their mother with chores. Yukye spent his free time mostly kicking stones. One day, a stone finally spoke up, asking, "Why do you always kick us? You kick us while hunting with your father, fetching water for your mother, and playing with your siblings. Do you hate us or love us, young man?" The stones had enough, and one brave stone confronted him, demanding an explanation for his relentless kicking.

Yukye was shocked when he discovered the Stone could actually talk! Grinning from ear to ear, Yukye poured his heart out to them, apologizing for any pain he may have accidentally caused. He eagerly asked if they could now be buddies. Yukye revealed that he kicked the Stones because he couldn't afford a soccer ball, but they were always his first choice. Both Yukye and the Stones were over the moon with their new bond. Yukye kept on kicking the Stones, showing off a talent that no other kids in Tena Village could even come close to. Despite others getting bumped and bruised when they tried kicking the stones, Yukye remained untouched, leaving everyone in awe of his incredible skills. As he carried on kicking and juggling the Stones, Yukye became a true legend in Tena Village!

Yukye went places because of kicking and juggling stones with incredible skill and finesse. His talent spread far and wide, reaching even the most distant villages. People started to refer to him as the Stone Soccer Baller, recognizing his unique abilities on the field. As he continued to showcase his exceptional talent, he caught the eye of a renowned soccer scout named Mister Nalada. Impressed by Yukye's raw talent and dedication, the scout extended an invitation for him to join his prestigious club in the north, promising to nurture and elevate him to the next level of success in professional soccer. Grateful for the opportunities that came his way, Yukye took a moment to express his gratitude for the Stones that had paved his path to fame. The Stones, in turn, felt a sense of pride and joy for Yukye's achievements, knowing that he was destined for greatness in the world of soccer. Though they would miss his presence, they were content knowing that Yukye was moving on to bigger and better things.

Kyeyuyu and Nagi were overjoyed for their son, and Yukwe's siblings were equally thrilled for him. The following day, bright and early on Monday morning, Yukwe meticulously packed his belongings into the trusty banana fiber bag and embarked on his journey to meet Coach Nalada. In those days, modern modes of transportation, such as cars, bicycles, trains, and ships, were non-existent. Yukwe trekked tirelessly for a considerable distance until he finally arrived at Dula Village. Dula Village marked the beginning of his promising soccer career, boasting more advancements than Tena Village and the surrounding communities. The beginning of something truly special!

The residents of Dula Village were overwhelmed with excitement upon Yukwe's arrival, eagerly requesting a display of his remarkable barefoot stone-kicking and juggling prowess. Bringing a special Stone from Tena Village as a symbol of their unbreakable bond, Yukwe astounded the audience with his impressive skills. Despite his primary focus on soccer, Yukwe graciously agreed to join the Dula Village Club for a period of five years while also pursuing his education. The club generously offered to cover his school fees and provide him with a substantial sum of ten silvers at the conclusion of each season, a considerable amount for that era. Yukwe was elated by this opportunity and chose to allocate a portion of his earnings toward the education of all eight of his siblings.

He used the money to build an amazing new house for Kyeyuyu and Nagi! Kyeyuyu and Nagi were absolutely thrilled about their son's soccer achievements. Yukye quickly bonded with his teammates on his very first day playing at Dula Village Club. He even became best friends with the talented twin brothers, Kala and Kalo, who were recruited from a neighboring village. The entire team was in awe of Yukye's skills, and he scored in every single game! His teammates and villagers adored him so much. Little did Yukye know some of his teammates were secretly jealous of his success. Sata, his opponent on the Dula Village team, grew so envious that he plotted to sabotage Yukye. But Coach Nalada always had Yukye's back and made sure he was the star player in every game, both at home and away matches.

Sata was certain about the Stone Yukwe had in his bag. It was a magical Stone that brought him good luck, helping him score goal after goal for the Dula Village Club. So Sata sneaked into Yukwe's bag, took the Stone, and hid it among a pile of identical stones, thinking Yukwe would never find it. Little did he know that Stone could talk! Before every game, Yukwe would open his bag, kiss the Stone, and then head out to play. During a crucial match against a neighboring village team, Yukwe couldn't find his precious Stone in his bag. Despite being distracted and worried, he decided to play the game and search for his friend later. Unfortunately, the Dula Village Club lost the game, as Yukwe's mind was preoccupied with thoughts of his missing friend. After the game, Yukwe searched frantically for his beloved Stone. He kicked and juggled each identical stone until he reached the last one. And then his friend let out a hearty laugh, bringing immense relief and joy to Yukwe's heart. He had finally found his cherished companion!

"You are not only a good kicker and juggler, but also a wise listener," said the Stone. When Yukwe finally found his lost voice, he couldn't help but laugh and express his relief at the Stone. He was overjoyed to have rediscovered it. Curious about how his friend ended up in the pile, Yukye listened intently as his friend recounted the events that led to their current situation. Promptly, Yukye sought out Sata and asked him to confess his misdeeds. Sata, in turn, apologized to Yukye and shared his true intentions regarding the stone. To everyone's astonishment, the Stone suddenly spoke up in front of Sata, imparting valuable wisdom about the futility of jealousy and hatred in problem-solving. Both Yukwe and the Stone encouraged Sata to dedicate himself to rigorous training in order to elevate his soccer skills. It was believed that through hard work, Sata could become a much better soccer player. Sata was taken aback by the stone's ability to communicate and expressed his gratitude for the invaluable advice given.

Yukye's journey was nothing short of incredible! With each passing season, he pushed himself to new heights, becoming a true master of the game. And when he decided to return to his hometown of Tena after a decade of professional success, he didn't just settle down—he took on the role of coach for the local village club! His passion and skill inspired countless children to join the sport and dream big. But Yukye's impact didn't stop there. The Stones he once kicked and juggled became a symbol of strength and stability, laying the foundation for buildings in the community. His legacy lives on, lifting his village and family out of poverty and moving them toward prosperity. Yukye's talent and dedication not only brought him fame but also brought hope and success to those around him. What a legend!

The End

THE BEAST CALLED DAMU

Once upon a time, in the mysterious forest of Ngamu, there dwelled a fearsome beast named Damu! This towering creature had a single eye in the middle of his face, striking terror into the hearts of the nearby villagers. They trembled at the mere thought of encountering him while searching for firewood. Despite numerous brave attempts by hunters to capture Damu, his incredible strength and lightning speed always eluded them. Meanwhile, in the same village lived the spirited family of Tapi, Darebu, and their four lovely daughters, Nija, Dite, Zemu, and the youngest, the captivating Razoe! Known for her breathtaking beauty and strong-willed nature, Razoe's infectious smile and kind heart won over everyone she met, despite her tendency to be a bit lazy. One fateful day, their parents sent the four daughters on a thrilling adventure into the heart of the Ngamu forest to gather firewood for their evening meal. Little did they know what amazing and daring escapades awaited them!

Tapi and Darebu excitedly asked them if they could go in the evening after the sun had set because in the afternoon there are many snakes in the Ngamu forest. Nija, Dite, Zemu, and Razoe eagerly listened to their parents and agreed to go in the evening when it was safer. At five o'clock, when the sun had gone down, the four daughters joyfully started walking toward the Ngamu forest, thrilled for their adventure. Nija, Dite, Zemu, and Razoe worked together with great enthusiasm to collect a lot of firewood that day, enjoying each other's company as they played "hide-and-seek" in the Ngamu forest and indulged in some delicious fruits they found. After a successful day of gathering firewood and having fun, the sisters began their journey back home, chatting and laughing along the way. However, as they were walking home, the skies suddenly opened up, and it started raining heavily, drenching them as they hurried home.

On the run to find shelter from the rain, they spotted a small house in the middle of the Ngamu forest. Nija, the oldest of the four sisters, instructed her siblings to seek refuge in the house. The sisters agreed and entered. As the rain began to subside, they heard a loud noise approaching the house. It was Damu, returning home from hunting with a large amount of meat. Nija, Dite, Zemu, and Razoe were terrified, their eyes wide open, as they all ran to hide in the corner of the house. They clung to each other tightly, trembling with fear, as Damu reached the door. In a booming voice, he exclaimed, "Am I mistaken? I smell humans in my house." Damu searched the corners of his home and spotted the frightened sisters in the left corner. In a reassuring tone, he said, "Don't be afraid. I won't harm you."

"How thrilled I am to have you lovely ladies here! You are always welcome in my humble abode. Shall we dine together this evening? It's almost eight o'clock, and the darkness of the forest is enveloping us. The towering trees are casting eerie shadows all around us." Damu prepared a delicious meal while the four sisters lent a helping hand. Once the meat was roasted, Damu served each sister a piece. Nija, Dite, and Zemu pretended to have eaten their meat, secretly hiding it away. But Razoe eagerly devoured hers, as she was famished. All four sisters spent the night at Damu's house. The next morning, they politely asked if they could return home, mentioning their worried parents. Damu rushed to the door, his single eye turning red and his mouthwatering.

He asked the four sisters for his pieces of meat back, the very ones he had generously shared with them during dinner that fateful night. The sisters felt a heavy weight of guilt and regret as they realized the magnitude of their actions. Nija, Dite, and Zemu, fueled by their deep-seated mistrust of Damu, had chosen to hold onto their portions of meat.

Damu's voice filled the room as he sang, pleading for the return of his rightful share: "Give me back my piece of meat. Give me back my piece of meat." Reluctantly, Nija, Dite, and Zemu handed over their pieces of meat, but it was too late for Razoe, who had already consumed hers. Damu's anger flared as he instructed Nija, Dite, and Zemu to leave, while Razoe was to stay behind. Fear gripped Razoe as she sang out a chilling warning, "Tell Dad and Mum that their beloved daughter, whom they cherish most, is about to become Damu the beast's next victim. Damu, step aside and let me go." The three sisters made their way back to the village, their hearts heavy with sorrow, carrying firewood on their heads, tears flowing freely, and their once-proud posture now slumped in anguish.

They were dejected about leaving their sister with Damu! Upon returning home, the three sisters eagerly shared every detail of their adventure with Tapi and Darebu. Tapi, Darebu, the sisters, and Chief Hasu of the village hurried back to the Ngamu forest to speak with Damu. To everyone's surprise, Damu requested a cow in exchange for companionship, as he was feeling lonely. Without hesitation, Tapi and Darebu agreed and gave him the cow. Damu reassured everyone that he meant no harm and just wanted a friend. Razoe happily embraced Damu and reunited with her family, and they all returned home with big smiles on their faces. Chief Hasu and the villagers no longer dreaded Damu, and the hunters stopped pursuing him. Razoe learned so much from her time with Damu, becoming more diligent, obedient, and patient. Damu and the villagers lived in perfect harmony from then on, forever. What a wonderful ending to an incredible story!

THE END

DANU, SON OF THE LIGHT

Once upon a time, there was a distant village called Mado. Mado Village was located on the north side of Gamu Village and thrived with rich fertile soil and farming activities, particularly the cultivation of Kafe, which was practiced by most members of the village. Chief Baku, a kind and generous leader, was the head of the royal family and the leader of the royal council in Mado Village. Danu and Nahu, important figures in Mado Village, also served on the royal council and actively participated in village decision-making. Alongside the royal council was the security council of Mado Village, known as Disa, responsible for maintaining law and order. Danu, a talented man, was believed to have had a miraculous life from birth. On the day Danu was born, Mado Village experienced two days without a sunset or sunrise, a phenomenon known as the "two-day light." This event remained a mystery to Danu's family and the villagers, but it marked the beginning of a life filled with miracles and mysteries for Danu.

Nahu was born in the same period, only two months after Danu. However, Nahu was not followed by the same miracles and mysteries as Danu. As they both grew up, Nahu was always jealous of Danu, for Danu was revered for his relationship with Gina. Danu lived the life of a fisherman, spending most of his time on Gasu

Lake. This meant Danu left home at sunrise and returned after sunset. Danu's wife was the most beautiful woman in Mado Village. Most villagers would compare her to an "African ghost" because of her beauty that radiated in sunlight. When Gina smiled, hearts were filled with joy and calm, for her smile was like that of Queen Sheba, and her warmth calmed even the harshest of hearts. Danu loved his wife more than anything in this world and never knew that Nahu was jealous of his relationship with Gina, as Nahu, too, felt he shared a love for her that he could not describe.

Danu, Nahu, and Gina grew up together in Mado Village. As children, they were inseparable and the best of friends, often referred to by others as the mischievous three. As they entered adolescence and adulthood, the dynamics of their relationship began to change as Gina and Danu fell in love. Unfortunately for Nahu, this sparked feelings of jealousy, as he also harbored feelings for Gina that were not reciprocated. Over the years, Nahu's jealousy grew to the point where he plotted against Danu in an attempt to sabotage him and his position on the Royal Council.

Nahu decided he would steal the royal statue from the royal house on the east side of Mado Village late at night when the guards were fewer and tired from a hot, sunny day. This royal statue had existed for nearly one thousand years and was seen in the village as a sacred heirloom to the royal family. The timing to steal the statue and place it inside Danu's and Gina's house was perfect, for Gina had gone to fetch firewood in the Kago forest, and Danu had gone fishing. With no one home, this was Nahu's perfect opportunity to take advantage. Shortly after sunset, he began his quest. First, he snuck into the royal house to collect the statue, then he entered Danu's house and hid the royal statue inside. When Chief Baku woke up early the next day, he went to the royal house for his daily spiritual prayer and was shocked to find everything disorganized, looking as if it had been hit by a tornado.

Chief Baku searched far and wide for the royal statue, but he could not find it. He immediately called for a royal meeting, and Nahu was the first to show up at the royal house while other elders followed. To Nahu's appeasement, Danu never attended because he was in the middle of Gasu Lake, completely unaware of the events unfolding. When the meeting started, Nahu was the first to stand up to speak to the royal council, and he suggested to Chief Baku that they check every elder's house in case the culprit was among them. Nahu even offered to be searched first, while the other elders followed. Chief Baku agreed with him because only the elders had access to the royal house, so their first look should be at those with the closest access.

With no luck finding the statue at Nahu's house, to no surprise of Nahu, the search continued to other elders' homes. Chief Baku eventually asked himself and the other elders why Danu had not come to the royal meeting, but no one gave an answer, leaving Chief Baku puzzled. Nahu gladly jumped in with the idea to search Danu's house next and told Chief Baku that Danu must be at his house. Upon arriving at Danu's house, Chief Baku and the elders found Gina just returning from fetching firewood. She was pleased to see Chief Baku, Nahu, and the royal elders at her house in the afternoon when it was so hot. Gina welcomed them all, and Nahu replied with a sweet voice, all the while disguising what he had done in trying to destroy Danu and separate him from Gina. Avoiding any small talk and with anger in his voice, Chief Baku immediately got to the point.

Gina, he said, "We are here at your home because of the lost royal statue, and we think someone who stole it was one of us. We are checking every royal elder's house." Gina was both startled by the news of the lost statue and surprised by the eagerness to check her and Danu's house as if they were being accused. In the blink of an eye, the Disa were already in the house, checking every corner from top to bottom. After at least a twenty-minute search that kept Gina in complete silence over the shock, they did not find the royal statue anywhere. Nahu overheard the Disa confirming with Chief Baku that the royal statue was not in the house. Nahu was secretly shocked and confused, given that he was certain the royal statue would be in the house. Chief Baku and the elders left Danu's house to continue their search, and Nahu spent the night overthinking what could have happened, for he was certain he had not placed the statue anywhere else but in Danu's house. He was convinced his plan would work, but little did Nahu know that his actions had been seen by the one woman he was trying to win over.

The day the royal statue went missing and Nahu played out his mischievous plot, Gina was walking back from the forest and witnessed Nahu running out of her house. After entering her home, she immediately felt that Nahu's presence there was not out of friendship or kindness as a friend just stopping by for a visit; rather, she knew something had been done, but she was not entirely sure what. She began searching all rooms of her house, looking for what she did not know, until she finally came across it—the royal statue she recognized from the royal palace. When Danu returned from his day of fishing, Gina eagerly recounted every detail of the shocking betrayal they had experienced. Overwhelmed by a mix of exhaustion and disbelief, the pair sat together to reflect on their options moving forward. After carefully considering their next move, they ultimately made the decision to hide the stolen item in the very home of the man who had originally taken it from the royal house—Nahu.

In the meantime, Chief Baku and Disa were thrilled to kick off a thorough investigation in search of the lost statue! Chief Baku rallied all the royal elders for an urgent meeting, stressing the importance of the investigation led by the skilled Disa agents. They were determined to leave no stone unturned, even looking into the elders and their spouses, including Danu and Gisa, as well as exploring leads outside the elders if necessary. When Nahu caught wind of the investigation, he couldn't help but feel a surge of nervous excitement, wondering what revelations would come to light, especially since the statue didn't turn up in Danu's home as he had hoped.

As part of the investigation, Disa introduced Jagugu, the secret animal they used to solve royal issues. Jagugu was a magical creature with three heads and the body of a dog. Its fur coat was speckled like that of a jaguar, and its tail was long like that of a cheetah. Jagugu had an incredibly strong sense of smell that could reach thirty yards and delve into disappearing nooks and crannies. Its hearing was impeccable, like that of a bat that relies only on sonic waves. Jagugu also had the intelligence and wisdom of an elephant because of its three heads. Many villagers feared Jagugu, not because it seemed furious but rather because they feared it could peer into the depths of their souls and uncover their most inner secrets with its impeccable senses. Due to this deep-rooted fear, Jagugu was commonly the last resort in any Disa investigation, only used when no other means could solve the puzzle.

Given the sensitive nature of the investigation, it began with a ceremonial drinking of the "dream water," as known by the villagers. All the royal elders came to the royal house and were given a watery drink from the far west of Mado Village. This drink induced even the deepest sleep in the most awake person, after which the investigation would commence. Chief Baku, Danu, Gina, Nahu, and all the royal elders drank the water, then immediately and peacefully fell into a deep sleep. The power of Jagugu's three minds had the ability to connect to the dreams of all those who drank the water. And as dreams often do, the elders began to dream about their lives in full, including the good and the bad, the truths and the secrets.

Jagugu commenced his investigation by methodically approaching each elder individually to delve into the depths of their dreams. Unsurprisingly, the majority harbored dreams centered around mundane topics such as life, marriage, and business. Eventually, Jagugu reached Danu, and with a reverent gesture, knelt beside him in a display of utmost respect. The same gesture was repeated with Gina, underscoring Jagugu's reverence and deference. The Disa observed with unwavering confidence in Jagugu's discernment as the subtle yet profound actions unfolded before them. Upon encountering Nahu, Jagugu astounded the Disa by unveiling Nahu's nefarious schemes against Danu and Gina, as well as his misguided affections for Gina, leading to potential sabotage. The shock only deepened as Jagugu turned his attention to Chief Baku, who was in a deep slumber on his royal chair. After intense concentration, Jagugu began barking at Chief Baku, prompting the Disa's alarm. Once again, Jagugu disclosed a startling revelation to the Disa: that the true chief of Mado Village was meant to be Danu, and Gina was meant to be the queen.

Jagugu had uncovered the long-held secret of the royal family. It was revealed that Chief Gado, the former leader, had two sons: Sako, who tragically perished in his youth during the war, and Baku, the sole surviving heir. However, what had been concealed for years was the fact that Baku was not actually a blood relative of Chief Gado. This revelation stemmed from a forbidden love affair between Chief Gado's wife and Nuhaha, Nahu's father. Concurrently, Chief Gado himself had a relationship with Giru, a woman of remarkable beauty and kindness who bore his true heir, Danu. For decades, Chief Gado kept this truth hidden to safeguard Danu from the wrath of the queen, whose opposition could imperil Mado Village. Prior to his demise, Chief Gado designated Danu as his rightful successor in his will. Yet, upon discovering this, the queen intervened, altering the will to ensure Baku's ascension to chiefdom.

Jagugu and Disa had discovered all the secrets, including the location of the royal statue. They retrieved the statue from Nahu's house and then called for an urgent village meeting in the square. All the elders were awoken, except for Danu, Gina, Nahu, and Chief Baku, as Disa wanted to address them first. The villagers were summoned and gathered in the center of Mado Village by daylight. The Disa began by informing the royal elders that Chief Baku was not the true chief of Mado Village, revealing that the real chief was Danu and Gina was the queen. The elders were taken aback and honored by the news, agreeing to awaken Danu and Gina and share the news with the entire village. Danu and Gina were astonished by the news and equally captivated by the sight of Disa, the warriors, and the Mado villagers now kneeling in respect to them as the new chief and queen of Mado Village, a humble man and woman, who were once a fisherman and a gatherer raised with simplicity and kindness.

At length, Nahu and Chief Baku were roused from their slumber, and Disa relayed the findings of the investigation. The discovery of the royal statue within Nahu's abode prompted a condemnation of his malevolent machinations against Danu. Overwhelmed by shame and regret, Nahu expressed remorse for his misguided actions, shedding tears of contrition. In a display of magnanimity, Danu, Gina, Disa, and the villagers of Mado opted to extend forgiveness to Nahu, albeit stripping him of his position on the royal council. Chief Baku, however, obstinately refused to acknowledge Danu as the new chief of Mado Village, clinging to the throne and rejecting the notion of a former fisherman assuming leadership. In deference to tradition, Danu agreed to partake in the ancient ritual set forth by generations of chiefs in times of discord. The challenge entailed each contender submerging a royal statue in a vessel of water, with the statue that floated representing the rightful chief.

Danu was the first to perform the task, followed by Baku. To Baku's astonishment, Danu's statue swiftly ascended to the surface, while Baku's sank to the depths, emitting only bubbles. The villagers erupted in jubilation, proclaiming "Danu, Danu, Danu." Thus, in accordance with the fables passed down through generations, the Son of Light ascended to the esteemed position of chief of Mado Village, with Gina as his queen. Disheartened by his defeat and consumed by disgrace, Baku sought solace in the Fahi Kingdom, aligning himself with the Hagi in the north. Revered for his wisdom, compassion, and adept problem-solving skills, Chief Danu emerged as one of the most esteemed leaders in the annals of Mado Village.

THE END

MR. BLUE BLOOM

Once upon a time, in the magical forest of Rabima, there was a family bursting with love led by the kindhearted Tapi and the talented Darebu! The couple had three stunning daughters, and their cozy home was tucked away on the peaceful east side of the forest. Tapi was a highly respected farmer in the nearby village, while Darebu's skills as a tailor were unmatched. Tapi poured his heart into his apple farm, while Darebu's creativity shone through in the beautiful dresses she made for their daughters and customers. The girls, in return, found delight in creating dresses for their dolls and spent endless hours playing with their mother's treasured tailoring machine. Nija, the eldest daughter, was enchanted by her vibrant orange dresses and had a fiery passion for dancing to traditional music. Dite, the middle child, thrived on the excitement of rope jumping and looked adorable in her elegant white dresses. Razoe, the youngest, had a deep love for music and was particularly fond of singing, solving puzzles, and twirling around in her beloved blue dresses!

Tapi and Darebu's daughters have the most exciting cleaning schedule ever! Each daughter gets to take charge of cleaning the house for two whole days a week, giving them a sense of responsibility and pride in maintaining their home. Nija diligently cleans on

Monday and Tuesday, ensuring everything is spotless and organized. Dite takes over Wednesday and Thursday, ensuring every nook and cranny is sparkling clean. Razoe, the youngest, tackles the cleaning duties on Friday and Saturday with a bit of help and encouragement from her supportive parents. And on Sundays, the whole family comes together for a cleaning party, making chores feel like a fun and bonding activity. Let's not forget about their super cool best friend, Mr. Blue Bloom, who has been a beloved part of the family for almost a decade, adding a touch of whimsy and charm to their home. With his blue appearance and friendly presence near the house door in the corner of the sitting room, Mr. Blue Bloom brings joy and laughter to the household. How delightful and heartwarming is that?

The entire family was overjoyed to have Mr. Blue Bloom assist with keeping the house clean! The daughters were especially enamored with his cleaning services. Nija and Dita were incredibly diligent and hardworking, always putting all their hearts into keeping the house spotless. Whenever Razoe, the youngest and most beautiful daughter, neglected her cleaning duties, her sisters would quickly step in to ensure the house remained immaculate. Razoe had a tendency to create messes, litter garbage everywhere, and fail to maintain the beauty of the home. However, one day Nija and Dita decided to visit Auntie Lomi in the city, leaving Razoe in charge of the house. At the same time, Tipa was busy tending to his cows and goats, while Darebu went to the neighboring town to deliver dresses to her customers.

Razoe was feeling extremely lethargic and overwhelmed by the thought of cleaning the house. As she let out a distressed cry for help, she pleaded, "I simply don't have the energy to tackle this mess. Could someone please lend me a hand?" Little did she know, Mr. Blue Bloom was eavesdropping from his cozy corner. Touched by Razoe's plea, he gently offered his assistance, saying, "My dear, I can help you with cleaning the house." To Razoe's astonishment, Mr. Blue Bloom not only spoke but also proposed a surprising deal. She couldn't help but question, "But how can a bloom like you speak?" It all seemed like a surreal dream to her, yet the offer of help was very real. With a sense of calm, Razoe agreed to let Mr. Blue Bloom assist her with the cleaning. In a twist of events, Mr. Blue Bloom cheekily asked, "If I help clean the house, will you promise to marry me when you're older?" Razoe was taken aback by the unexpected proposal. With a bright smile, she responded, "Yes, I promise to marry you, Mr. Blue Bloom." And so, a heartfelt promise was made between Razoe and Mr. Blue Bloom, a vow they both swore never to break.

In the blink of an eye, he had already finished cleaning the house, leaving it looking spotless and fresh. As Tapi, Darebu, Nita, and Dita walked through the front door, they were taken aback by the immaculate condition of their home. It was Razoe who broke the news that Mr. Blue Bloom was responsible for the cleaning and that he had the ability to speak. The shock on everyone's faces was palpable, and they all eagerly anticipated hearing Mr. Blue Bloom speak once more. Slowly, Mr. Blue emerged from his secluded corner and warmly greeted everyone present. Razoe then surprised Tapi, Darebu, and her sisters by revealing her intention to marry Mr. Blue when she turned twenty. The unexpected turn of events left Tapi, Darebu, and their daughters bewildered and intrigued by what the future held.

Tipa, Darebu, and the sisters were eagerly anticipating Razoe's opinion once again. With overwhelming excitement, Razoe exclaimed, "I have made the decision to marry Mr. Blue Bloom!" To everyone's amazement, Mr. Blue Bloom magically transformed into a handsome man right before their very eyes. The family was left speechless by the incredible transformation that unfolded before them. Mr. Blue Bloom wasted no time and started working on the farm for Tipa and Darebu, patiently waiting for Razoe to come of age. As the years went by, Razoe blossomed into a kind and breath-taking young woman.

Finally, in a beautiful ceremony held at the farm, Razoe and Mr. Blue Bloom exchanged vows. Their marriage was a whirlwind of happiness and love as they embarked on a blissful life together. Two years into their marriage, Razoe discovered she was pregnant, and they joyfully welcomed baby Nihaka into their growing family.

THE END

ABOUT THE AUTHOR

Martin Muganga was born and raised in Kampala District, Uganda. He attended Makerere University, where he graduated with a degree in community psychology. In his mid-twenties, he met his wife, Ann Louise Tezak, who was doing research in Uganda at the time. In 2011, Martin immigrated from Uganda to the United States to marry his wife and begin their lives together. Martin first lived in Montana, Florida, and Tennessee, where his daughter was born before his wife became a diplomat and his family joined the foreign service. Their first assignment overseas has been in Porto Alegre, Brazil, where they reside. In Martin's free time, he enjoys playing soccer, swimming, reading, watching the news, watching movies, and spending time with his family.